*What has to happen before you really connect
with God in a worship service?
How do you get all participants—
those up in front and those in the pew—
totally involved in worship?*

*Go step by step with the author
through a worship service from the viewpoints
of the minister, the organist, the choir
director, the choir, the ushers,
and the people in the pews.
Then, if you keep on playing church,
you'll know what you're missing.*

Up with Worship

BY ANNE ORTLUND

A Division of G/L Publications
Glendale, California, U.S.A.

Scripture quotations unless otherwise noted
are from *The Living Bible*, Copyright © 1971
by Tyndale House Publishers, Wheaton, Illinois.
Used by permission.

© Copyright 1975 by G/L Publications
All rights reserved

Second Printing, 1977

Published by
Regal Books Division, G/L Publications
Glendale, California 91209
Printed in U.S.A.

Library of Congress Catalog Card No. 74-32329
ISBN 0-8307-0354-3

Contents

Dedicated to my pastor,
a godly man whose life and words
constantly urge me to Christ.
I'm so lucky—
I'm even married to him.

Part One

LET'S TALK ABOUT CHURCH

1

IS YOUR CHURCH
FOR REAL?
Settle down for a really honest yes or no.

When I was little we used to play church. We'd get the chairs into rows, fight over who'd be preacher, vigorously lead the hymn singing, and generally have a great carnal time.

The aggressive kids naturally wanted to be up front, directing or preaching. The quieter ones were content to sit and be entertained by the up-fronters.

Occasionally we'd get mesmerized by a true sensationalistic crowd-swayer—like the girl who said, "Boo! I'm the Holy Ghost!" But in general, if the up-fronters were pretty good they could hold their audience quite a while. If they weren't so good, eventually, the kids would drift off to play something else—like jump rope or jacks.

Now that generation has grown up, but most of them haven't changed too much. Every Sunday they still play church. They line up in rows for the entertainment. If it's pretty good, their church may grow. If it's not too hot, eventually they'll drift off to play something else—like yachting or wife swapping.

———————————

Not often do churchgoers find themselves in the Presence!

But when they do—

All is changed. They may destroy their idols, as in Genesis 35:2.

They may, as a group, promise to obey all of God's Word, as in Exodus 24:7.

They may have a great musical time, as in 2 Chronicles 5:11-14.

They may be moved to weeping, as in Nehemiah 8:9.

They may just have a wonderful "ball" enjoying God! In Nehemiah 8:6 they said, "Amen," lifted their hands toward heaven and then bowed and worshiped with their faces toward the ground.

In any case, they are moved to *move!* Repent—weep—rejoice—*something!* When God is present in power, if the people don't respond the very stones will.

———————————

I don't know about you. If you've never been in church when God was obviously present, may this book make you so thirsty for that to happen, you'll be absolutely cotton-mouthed.

If you have—do you remember? Stop and recall. Oh, holy, glorious, sweaty-palms time! If you were the leader, you wondered when—how—if you should put a lid on this bubbling pot!

One thing is sure: you knew, "Oh, God, this is what

3

I was made for. This is stretching and rewarding and fulfilling, down deep in my bones. This is Eternity Business. I'm being caught up into the Important."

This is—breaking into glory!

_____

After that, you will never again be satisfied to just play church.

2

ON THE STREET
WHERE WE LIVE
We're the very ordinary, being visited
by the Extraordinary.

All I can tell about is what I know myself.

Our church is Lake Avenue Congregational Church in Pasadena, California. It happens to be a bubbling pot these days. (Lord, keep the fire hot.)

What's it like? We call Lake Avenue a "Conglomerational Church." The pastor, my husband Ray, is an ex-Presbyterian minister. Others are ex-everything: Baptist, Methodist, Presbyterian, whatever. We baptize every way, every age: "Don't stress the ritual," says Ray; "stress the real. The Holy Spirit is placing us in the body of Christ."

The three morning services are fairly formal, with attendance totaling maybe 2200. The evening service is informal—with 600 to 1000 attending. Music is Bach to rock; races, many; age-span, wide. Pasadena is the Rose Bowl, the Rose Parade, Cal Tech. . . . Our kids wear shoes.

So how does our particular "pot" bubble?

Most often, just slightly under simmer—with movement, aliveness just under the surface. The people listen aggressively, murmur comments sometimes, turn Bible pages to follow the sermon and many take notes. They are quick to laugh, quick to sober up. "Fun to preach to!" says Ray.

But the pot's ready to boil at any time, the hearty singing gives it away. And the occasional services of really High Praise (like Easter Sunday evenings) are really High Praise.

The best Sunday evening services are feedback times when the Body talks to itself. Young and old at microphones line up to report what God is doing in their lives, to confess, to exhort, to chuckle.... It's sometimes hard to turn off the faucet at the end.

During the week hundreds of small groups "do the work of the ministry," discipling and being discipled. Brothers and sisters are committed to lunching together, praying over the phone, grouping in living rooms, bearing one another's burdens.*

There's life—life that spreads over the world through 86 missionaries and through more than a million dollars a year—out of our 2800 pockets.

What makes Lake Avenue happen?

Well, we certainly haven't "arrived." We say, "What's the Holy Spirit doing today? Let's do *that*. Where's the Holy Spirit going today? Let's go *there*. What can we do—*in this day*—to bring God and people together?"

In this day!

A living church is a contemporary one; it isn't trying to be twenty years ahead—strained and strange.

It isn't content to be twenty years behind—musty and dusty.

A living church gathers up all of its age groups and says, "Come! In this precious, unique, 'now' time, let's all together go hard after God!"

* See *Lord, Make My Life a Miracle!* by Raymond C. Ortlund, Regal Books, G/L Publications, 1974.

3

**WORSHIPING
IN THE NOW**
**You've got to fit into this particular
slice of God's eternity.**

Let me describe what Pentecost *wasn't* like, all right?
Picture all those believers meeting together; suddenly
there's the sound of a mighty rushing wind and it fills
all the house where they're sitting.

"Great! This is wonderful!" they cry. "Quick! Shut the
windows! Let's capture this glorious wind forever!"

So twenty, thirty years later, there they sit—faces
flushed, eyes glazed, remembering the day God came—
and determined to keep everything exactly as it was
then. . . .

My friend, the wind is a *wind*. You can't trap it, you
just have to go with it. Thus it is with the Holy Spirit!

Past successes can completely undo you, Christian, and
undo your church, too. God blessed something so won-
derfully a while back; it was so beautiful; so you work
at it, you fan it, you wear out the saints trying to revive
it. But, friend, God has gone on to something else—and
you don't even know it!

7

Forget yesterday; today is God's precious gift. His name is "I AM." He is forever contemporary. Christians who stay with Him are the same—they're happy, "now" people. Churches who stay with Him are happy, "now" churches. "The old is gone; the new has come" (2 Cor. 5:17). "Forgetting the past, they press on to what lies ahead" (Phil. 3:13).

They stay current because God is current, and they're with Him! They have a built-in sloughing-off process, by which the worn-out gets eliminated.

How is it with you, Christian? Have you taken a day off lately to get alone with God and fast and pray and say, "What in my life needs to go? What has 'had it'? What new good thing needs to be strengthened or added?"

How is it with your church? When the Body comes together to worship God, do you ask, "What's gotten dreary? What needs to go? What needs to be freshened, changed? What needs to be added? Where are we as a people? What are our needs? What would be great for God? How can we all together connect with Him—in *this* world—*today?*"

4

WORSHIP SERVICES
CAN'T BE SERVED SMORGASBORD
"Let me see: shall I have contemporary
or traditional today?"

The game plan for this book is that it deals with the local church, maybe *your* church, in how to bring life out of deadness—in how to make the worship service a happening. So sometimes it talks to pastor, sometimes to organist, sometimes to a person in the pew, sometimes to choir director. But everybody needs to know the philosophy behind what everybody else is doing; so everybody needs to read all of the game plan, right?

One thing we learn about God's dealing with people is that He does it in *togetherness.*

The children of Israel moved *together* across the wilderness. (That wasn't always easy.)

The young, vigorous ones probably wanted to go twice the pace.

The young mothers with babies and toddlers needed to take it easy.

The oldest probably never wanted to move at all.

It took a lot of give and take, a lot of consideration for the condition of the other fellow, a lot of accommodating. But when it was all over, except for those who died along the way, they all got from *here* to *there*—together.

They all obeyed the sight of cloud and fire, the sound of trumpets.

They grumbled and were punished together—but together they also saw waters part, rods bud, and fire come out of heaven.

They knew each other well. They did it all together.

—————————

Pastor, in however long a time God gives you with your people—three years, thirty years—you have to get your people from here to there, together. Lead them together. Help them feel *all one*. The pagan deity Janus was two-faced: one face looked forward and the other looked back. A congregation will become two-faced when the conservatives attend the one consistently "straight" service while the "progressives" experiment with the latest in contemporary.

No, no! Put elements of both old and new in whatever the people experience, but pace your people to go forward experiencing everything together.

Some older ones will grumble.

Some younger ones will want to cavort more.

Expect both reactions and help them be considerate of each others' feelings.

Do you have several morning services? Try to make them identical so that there will be a wide spread of ages in each service. Preach the same sermon each time.

Give them the feeling when it's all over that they grumbled and endured together, but they saw some glory together, too. Together they all lost some of the old; together they all gained some of the new; but they all were a Body together—conservatives and progressives struggling to put it together—together!

After all, every car must have both gas and brakes. That's the very way it gets from here to there.

5

THREE CHEERS
FOR STIFF, RIGID ROWS OF PEWS!
Alternatives may become humanistic.

This is the age of stress on "relationships." I'm-okay-you're . . . et cetera. Everyone is so lonely—that's why we're reaching out.

We're discovering fellowship and it's great. When we discover worship, it will be greater.

We're discovering "Body life," and that's essential. But we haven't yet gazed too long at the Head. Thank the Lord for small groups! Circles of friends gathered in His name are wonderful. They bring me out of myself to others.

But better than being us-centered is being God-centered. Better than circles is being shoulder to shoulder—whether standing, sitting, kneeling or on our faces. Better than "sharing" is worshiping—aware of one another only in that deep, joyous awareness of being caught up together in God.

Eyes—minds—hearts "front and center"!

People say, "But rows are so impersonal." Exactly!

Jesus took His very dearest friends with Him up the mountain to pray.

But then He withdrew from them a stone's throw.

6

THE CHURCH SERVICE
IS A STAGE PLAY
Who's in the spotlight?

So the people all come together in rows in the church, and they face forward. So what?

Well, it's the same physical setup as a stage play, and everybody knows about *those*. You plunk down in a seat. . . . At H-hour the lights go up; the actors start performing, a prompter offstage whispers cues—and the spectators lean back and evaluate how they do.

But church? NO, NO, NO, NO, NO, NO, NO!

Church is unique. Whether the people in the congregation ever discover it or not, *they* are the actors. The up-front people are the prompters, whispering cues as needed—and God is the Audience, looking on to see how they do.*

Many poor churches don't even know who's supposed to be *doing it!* What lousy, lousy plays they put on! The actors sit around lethargically while the prompters practically exhaust themselves trying to do all their lines for them so the play will still give a lively appearance.

It doesn't.

---

* Kierkegaard said it first, I didn't. But that analogy has really helped me. Maybe it will you.

Nobody is fooled.

Pastor, minister of music, organist, what are you so self-conscious for? Do you think you're in the spotlight? You're not. Quit posturing! Just get down on your knees, and ask God to stimulate you and your people together to start performing.

7

BROKEN BOTTLES
How do you get a congregation going?

Dear up-front people! Are you really burdened about that flock of yours? Do you care? Do you see them as just an impossible bunch?

A while back, Ray preached on Mark 14:3. "Here came Mary," he said, "with her alabaster vase of nard to the dinner where Jesus was. She broke the bottle and poured it on Him."

An alabaster vase—milky white, veined, smooth, precious.

And pure nard inside! Gone forever. According to John 12:3, the whole house became filled with the fragrance.

Some story.

Christians file into church on a Sunday morning. One by one by one they march in—like separate alabaster vases.

Contained.

Self-sufficient.

Encased.

Individually complete.

15

Contents undisclosed.

No perfume emitting at all.

Their vases aren't bad looking. In fact, some of them are the Beautiful People, and they become Vase-Conscious: conscious of their own vase and of one another's. They're aware of clothes, of personalities, of position in this world—of exteriors.

So before and after church (maybe during) they're apt to talk Vase Talk. *Your ring is darling; what stone is that? Did you hear if Harry got that job? What is Lisa's boy doing for the summer? Is that all your own hair? I may take tennis lessons if George wants to.*

———————————

Mary broke her vase.

Broke it?! How shocking. How controversial. Was everybody doing it? Was it a vase-breaking party? No, she just did it all by herself. What happened then? The obvious: all the contents were forever released. She could never hug her precious nard to herself again.

———————————

Many bodies who file into church, no doubt, do so because they have Jesus inside of them. Jesus!—precious, exciting, life giving. But most of them keep Him shut up, contained, enclosed all their lives. And the air is full of NOTHING. They come to church and sit—these long rows of cold, beautiful, alabaster vases! Then the cold, beautiful, alabaster vases get up and march out again, silently—or maybe talking their cold alabaster talk—to repeat the ritual week after week, year after year.

Unless they just get too bored and quit.

The need for Christians everywhere (nobody is exempt) is to be broken. The vase has to be smashed! Christians

16

have to let the life out! It will fill the room with sweetness. And the congregation will all be broken shards, mingling together for the first time.*

Of *course* it's awkward and scary to be broken! Of *course* it's easier to keep up that cold alabaster front.

It was costly for Mary, too.

When Ray preached on Mark 14:3, I wrote on a card, "Lord, break my strong will, my argumentativeness, my quickness to reach decisions ahead of others and always think I'm right, my desire to have my opinion always considered. I'm sure I'm often obnoxious, Lord—maybe embarrassing to Ray. Forgive me, and help my fervent spirit be converted into just being fervent in loving You, fervent in joy, fervent in peace, et cetera. Lord, break me. Thank You for doing it! Amen."

We see the same truth in other Scriptures. In John 12:24,25 that hard, closed-up seed with precious life inside has to fall into the ground and die before the life can spring up. In 2 Corinthians 4:6,7 the clay vessel has light inside, but who could ever see light through a clay pot? Do you know what happens to a roomful of Christians when all the clay pots get broken at once? What glory! What light!

What is the need as people come together as a congregation? It is for them to be broken together.

"The high and lofty one who inhabits eternity, the Holy One . . ." (How do I get there, Lord?) ". . . says

---

* I remember that when God broke us all together at Wheaton College in February 1970, one of the students said it was like Orientation Week all over again: they were beginning to get to know one another.

this: I live in that high and holy place where those with contrite, humble spirits dwell; and I refresh the humble and give new courage to those with repentant hearts."*

The way to up is down!

The Holy One lives among broken people!

Christian, break your vase. Help your brothers and sisters break theirs. Split those exteriors. Have a smashing time. Then life will begin to mingle and flow around you and fill the whole church with the fragrance of Jesus!

When vases get broken, vase-awareness goes. The wealthy tennis player has his arm around the asthmatic stamp collector. The black high-school boy joshes freely with the wheeler-dealer car salesman. Spirits commune with spirits. Interiors and exteriors mingle unselfconsciously, because whole people are talking to whole people.

Your ring is darling; what stone is that? . . . I praise the Lord for the look on your face as you sang that hymn this morning. . . . Did you hear if Harry got that job? I was asking God to encourage him this week, one way or another. . . . What is Lisa's boy doing for the summer? . . . I just have to tell you what I found in Isaiah 6 this morning. . . . You must pray for me; the old temper really flared up yesterday. . . . I appreciate you, sister; thanks for ministering to my daughter this week. You said what I couldn't say. . . .

The nard fills the air. Beautiful! Take a deep breath.

If you know one another as broken people, you're ready to get on with a church service.

* Isaiah 57:15, *The Living Bible.*

18

8

WHEN LAKE AVENUERS GOT BROKEN
We discovered that God is the God of the desperate.

Ray and I had left our congregation five times to minister in far-off places. Each time our own flock prayed around the clock for us, as they do whenever we go. (People sign up for 15-minute prayer periods, night and day, during the period of ministry. They'll never, never know what that support means to us.) In the summer of 1972 they began to show frustration.

Ray had been pastoring the only Christian church in Afghanistan for three months. We came back with stories of how the Holy Spirit had broken through in power in that little struggling church, reviving His people. At the time we didn't know the reason for this special revival, but it was to prepare for persecution to come.

Our people said, "We pray for other people around the clock and they experience revival. Why don't we pray for ourselves?" So in June the dear people prayed around the clock. And what happened was . . . they just prayed around the clock. Nothing else special. Was God teaching us that He was not a bellboy who would jump every time the buzzer sounded? But for years prayer groups prayed specifically for revival. Surely He was not turning a deaf ear—?

Again in December the flock prayed continuously as Ray and I saw missionaries in Peru meet the Lord in a fresh way through many hours of tears, joy, confession, repentance, and glory.

This increased frustration for Lake Avenuers.

Ray and I talked to God.

"Dear Lord, six times You've been so gracious to us. Shouldn't the seventh time, the perfect number, be with our own congregation, the ones we love the most?"

Then we prayed some more: "O Father, Jacob served fourteen years for Rachel. This is our fourteenth year of labor at Lake Avenue Church. Why shouldn't this be reward year?" Then we tried a new tack: "Lord, this is Lake Avenue's seventy-seventh year as a church; and *You* know about sevens. . . ."

Meanwhile Ray was probing. In each of the six ministries where we'd seen God meet His people in an unusual way there seemed to be only one common ingredient: time. There would be different ages, different circumstances—sometimes the people knew each other well, sometimes not at all. But they'd all had time: time to wait before God, time to linger with one another in His presence.

Ray decided that our church service format programmed out any unusual working of God. On television, every problem had to be solved in 29 or 58 minutes. In church, we were open for all God would do for us in an hour and ten minutes, but after *that*—

In January Ray called for a Week of Waiting on God. There would be nothing happening: no boards, no committees, no midweek prayer meeting, no Sunday School class affairs. . . . Many people, bless 'em, even postponed social engagements.

We would just meet to wait on God. There would

20

be no program, nothing planned, we would just gather and *wait*. On Monday night we would wait on Him as families in our homes. Beginning Tuesday night, we would meet at church. . . .

Seven-thirty Tuesday was Heart-in-Throat Time. Would anybody come? The downstairs began to fill. The balconies began to fill. Soon the sanctuary was practically full. "You announce some big-name speaker and you hope for a crowd. You just tell 'em God's going to be here, and wow—"

Each evening some of us met for an hour or more ahead of time to pray and to throw ideas into the hopper.

"Let's study the Seventy-third Psalm in groups of twos and threes for a while. . . ."

"Let's sit quietly and let anyone lead out in singing and we'll join in. . . ."

"Let's walk out in silence tonight. . . ."

Each evening Ray and other brothers went into the sanctuary armed with maybe a dozen ideas, to use all or none. But they sat back, and mostly, the spirit of the people just pushed things along. Unless a change of pace seemed called for, people most often just lined up at the mike to share Christ. This was nothing new. But the spirit of brokenness and openness and confession was new. There were tears, there was laughter. It was something else.

We learned that waiting on God involves waiting for one another. We learned patience for the Body. We learned to honor the "lesser" members, whose right to participate probably exceeded, if anything, the others. Love in practical form!

Those with the hour-and-ten-minute clock inside them slipped away, but hundreds tasted the sweet fruits of what God does for those who *wait on Him*.

Wednesday night Ray told us about alabaster vases. (He talked very little all week.) A lot of us turned a corner that night. One woman discovered a broken vase on her floor at home, and kept it there untouched for the rest of the week, as a symbol of her own spirit.

Perhaps the high point was Friday evening for a couple of hours around midnight. One of the teen-agers said, "You know, I've dreamed of the time when I'd see the entire congregation on their knees in prayer—just filling the whole sanctuary."

Nobody could have planned it. We all went to our knees. For perhaps two hours the air was full of praise. Sometimes people prayed, adoring Him. Sometimes spontaneously we sang to Him.

From the little tastes of revival we've seen, when God and His people connected in very special ways, Ray and I have noticed several things:

No two situations are ever alike. God doesn't run out of ideas, but it's true that God's presence is such a cleansing fire, confession and repentance are always there. We have come to the conclusion that the Holy Spirit is a Gentleman. We have never seen excesses in behavior. He is *seemly!* But we've seen His characteristics exhibited in living color: great tenderness, great compassion for those embarrassed by their own sin, lots of tears but also lots of fun.

In my Bible I have the date January 26, 1973, marked beside Isaiah 25:9:

"This is our God, . . . for whom we waited. Now at last he is here!" (*TLB*).

9

LEADERS
MUST OFTEN FOLLOW FOLLOWERS
How else can Christ bring
His Body together in humility?

Several years ago we were kneeling on cushions around a long, low dining table in a private hotel suite in Japan. The air was seasoned with celery and leeks and unknown things.

Through a missionary interpreter, an important Japanese industrialist was addressing Ray:

"I have come to this city and invited you to join our family at dinner so that I might ask you a question. During the past year my son has become a Christian. I admit that he was rebellious and hard to handle, and now he is a respectful, good boy. But as you know, Christians in Japan are a very small minority and are looked down upon as being low-class, disloyal both to family and to country.

"There are so many sons in Japan. Why would this have to happen to *my* son—to *me?*"

God suddenly gave the translating missionary a tender parable.

"Suppose," he said, "a shepherd wanted to take his flock to better pastures. But the way was across a raging stream, and one ram was particularly frightened and refused to budge. How would he get that dear sheep to make the trip? Why, he would take his lamb, his precious lamb, and put it on the other side first. . . ."

We watched the father's lined face as understanding dawned. A tear ran down his cheek. "Ah, so," he said.

There's almost always some trailblazer out in front of the supposed "leader." The children are ahead of their parents. Some praying person in the church is ahead of the pastor. The young people are ahead of the adults.

Of course, the "big ones" can always choose to be proud and critical and defensive.

Or they can say, "Show me. Teach me what you know. I'm such a little child, but I want all of God in Jesus Christ that I can get. I want Him in knowledge and I want Him in experience. Help me. Pray for me. Disciple me, until I get to where you are."

Oh, how hard, how rare, how sweet!

It's a funny thing. A congregation of people doesn't become broken because the minister tells them to.

They get broken when *he* gets broken.

Part Two

NOW LET'S GO THROUGH
A WORSHIP SERVICE

10

WHO'S RESPONSIBLE
FOR THIS THING, ANYWAY?
Somebody has to make the first move.

How many people have to get hungry for their church service to become a Happening—before it happens?

Well, I've heard the same story you have about Dwight L. Moody—how he wasn't much until two old ladies in his congregation cried to God for him. They became the lever behind the scenes that moved the up-front person to move the people to God.

If you're a lay person reading this and you're burdened for your church, get together with a sympathetic heart and pray and pray. But watch it! Pray in sympathy and tenderness and great love; pray with an uncritical spirit; and pray that you'll be the first one changed! Then add to your prayers a life of faithful service, regular attendance, support, and optimism that God is at work answering your prayers. No bitterness, just agony and ecstasy!

And who are the up-front people who have to get concerned? This is only my own personal thinking; try it on for size:

Do you lead "two or three gathered together"? Or teach

a Bible class, a Sunday School class? Then you're up-front. You're the "pastor." No shifting of the weight to anybody else.

Or is yours a small church/group with two up-fronters, a pastor/teacher and a pianist, maybe organist? Then it will take both of you.

Suppose you're a medium-to-large church with pastor, minister of music, and organist. Then all three are your irreducible minimum.

Maybe you're First Church Downtown. You have several ministers regularly leading the worship service, plus minister of music, organist, and four paid soloists.

Then—like the sons of Kohath, all of you as a team are to bear the weight of the holy things of the tabernacle.*

And what does that tell you about up-front people? Well, you wouldn't call a spiritually weak person to be your pastor just because of his speaking gifts. Then neither will you call a spiritually weak person to be your church musician. No, no! Secular performances go down the street in the concert hall.

It takes all of these hearts, beating together, to make the service take wings and soar. Not because of great talent, maybe *in spite of* great talent. But just because it takes God's power to put people's hearts together—and that's the same power that raises a church service from the dead.

———————

And when you get together, what's to be your common goal?

* When the Israelites moved forward in the wilderness, there were plenty to oversee the carts and the beasts; but the Kohathites' lot was to bear the most sacred things personally on their shoulders (Num. 4:1-15).

It won't be to follow an order of service with a minimum number of goofs—to become a Smoothly Synchronized Team of Performers.

(Presenting, for Your Pleasure
on Sunday Mornings
the Incomparable
Rudolpho, Irena, and Dorothea)

Your common goal—along with choir, ushers, whoever—is nothing less than to connect the people with God Himself.

Holy.

Thrilling.

Cleansing.

Warming!

Possible.

Veni, Spirite Sancte. Oh, yes, God, do come, *please.*

Come to think of it, why settle for less? Isn't that what church is supposed to be all about?

But looking around the scene, maybe that's not such a common goal. It seems to be rather *un*common.*

---

* If the up-front people aim at nothing, they can be sure they'll hit it every time.

11

THE BUCK STOPS HERE
With the up-fronters.

Is it fair, is it scriptural, to put the burden of responsibility for the church squarely on its leadership? What about the ministry of the Body? What about the priesthood of all believers?

Well, without getting into the old chicken-and-egg question, I notice that when Christ sent messages to the seven churches in the book of Revelation, He sent them through the pastors (the "angels," the messengers of the Word). He considered them very key.

I know what it is, occasionally on vacation, to attend a church where the pastor has no charisma, where you just have hymns-announcements-offering-message, and nothing comes off through it all.

"What *is* the matter, Ray?" I whispered once into his ear.

"He has no theology of worship," Ray whispered back.

29

"Theology of worship!" Oh, right. There was no High and Holy One who was being pointed to and adored and confessed to and bowed down before.

The singing droned, "I was sinking deep in sin. . . ." We were certainly sunk deep in *something*.

Yes, it's fair to put the burden on the up-fronters.

They've got to care.

They've got to cry.

They've got to bang on the gates of heaven.

They've got to pound the Throne.

They've got to accept on their backs the Burden of the Lord.

12

THOSE BEAUTIFUL WORDS,
"BUT THE LORD—!"
There can be glory in the pew.

Maybe chapter 11 discouraged you. You sit every Sunday through one of those nothing-comes-off church services.

Dear friend! At this point you need to remember those great old words of George Fox:

"It is a wonderful discovery to find that you are a temple, that you have a church inside of you, where God is. In hushed silence, attend to Him. The Lord is in His holy temple."

You're sitting in church: before the service, confusion or silent sterility; during the service, well-meaning but corny slapstick. Or coldness, polished to a high glaze. Or just gray, dreary sameness. Or whatever your particular church problem is.

Do you feel that your church situation is a problem? Any time in life when you have a problem, put the problem up beside God. Then compare and see who's bigger. The book of Jonah starts out in a mess, when a man of God wasn't behaving right. Then verse 4 says, "BUT THE LORD . . . !" GOD WAS BIGGER! And God was moving.

So you don't care for the worship in your church? Well, it isn't the "worship" you're to worship; it isn't the minister or the music—it's God. Is He in your heart? Then, apart from anything that's happening up front, out back, around you, anywhere—you can have your own private breakthrough into glory!

Oh, my friend, He waits to be all in all to you. He is sufficient. You and He in a worship service together? That's enough.

Think of all the places in the world where Christians can't meet in His name at all. Be humble, be grateful, be sweetened in your soul. A critical spirit won't bring the glory.

Does that mean be tolerant, be satisfied with the present state of things? No, no! Behind the scenes, agonize in prayer for that beloved church of yours. Find another heart that beats with yours with revival (and who knows how to love and not criticize) and the two of you pray and don't quit.

But in church? Don't wait for "someday," and miss Him. You're there, He's there! Hooray! Three cheers for God! Sing! Pray! Celebrate! Let your face reflect the Presence!

Your personal worship doesn't depend on anybody else's behavior.

13

**MEANWHILE,
BACK BEHIND THE SCENES
If a church is going to have heart,
the printed bulletin has to, too.**

An organ prelude obviously doesn't fall together on a Sunday morning. It's been chosen and worked over quite a while before.

Neither does a meaningful pastoral prayer fall together on a Sunday morning. If the minister hasn't thought it through ahead of time, pretty soon he'll be praying the same things over and over, using the same clichés. . . .

What I'm working up to is that a worship service doesn't fall together on the spot, either. Unless it's been prayed through, discussed, and thought out in advance, before long it will be dull and repetitious.

God help the poor congregation who at any given point in a service can predict with accuracy what will happen ten minutes later!

Now, the order of worship in the bulletin will deal a death blow to the service if its purpose is just to make all those accurate predictions.

33

An order of worship isn't to program the up-front people! ("At this time the senior minister will pray; now the assistant minister will announce the offering," et cetera.)—which they read and dutifully obey while everybody watches.

Actually, relatively few are involved up front, and they can have their own notes on who's going to do what.

An order of worship should program the hearts of the congregation! "Now we're going to be sorry for our sins*. . . . Now we will sing hymn number 121, and then we will confess to God our faults. . . ."

This gives a new concept as to who is under pressure to read the order of worship and obey—both the up-front people *and* the congregation—while *God* watches.

And let your order of worship give more "heart" than details. If you print "choral response," then the choir is locked into it, and everybody knows it. Let the choir be prepared—but maybe when the time comes, God wants the people to respond in some way—to recite the Lord's Prayer, to pray in silence, to sing, "Spirit of the Living God. . . ." If you print "Response of Commitment" or something, you're freer—and the people are more apt to be on their toes in alertness and expectation.

Sometimes give the people little surprises. Let them not know who's going to take what. (The up-fronters know perfectly; they thought it all out in the pre-service huddle—but those are *their* secrets.) And tuck in small extras that aren't printed at all. (After you've prayed for new missionaries just going out, a soloist sings as a response, "So Send I You." After you've prayed particularly for our country, the choir sings softly in unison the refrain of "America.")

* Yes, it's biblical to program that: Leviticus 23:26-32.

Give the people special cues, through the order of worship, for behavior. How to spend the 10 minutes ahead of the service. How to pray for the ushers, the first-time guests, the choir. Tuck in a poem, a quotation, a Scripture verse to stimulate the flow of their thinking on the emphasis of the worship service.

Keep them moving along. Keep them *together*, through the order of worship: now we are all praising God; now we are all thinking about what we will give Him today. . . . We're thinking of Christ particularly now as our Shepherd, or our Redeemer, or our coming Lord.

We have a theme. We're moving along, going somewhere. Have you all caught it? Are we all together?

14

SPONTANEITY
IS NOT MORE SPIRITUAL
Practiced-in-advance
worship is just as biblical.

Where does the idea come from that if you're "in the Spirit" you can eliminate preparation?

I'm not unsympathetic to the philosophy behind it. If the Holy Spirit is a Wind, too quickly we get rigid and un-blowable. (Do something three Sundays in a row, and it's a Sacred Tradition.)

But all of our ideas of worship must be rooted firmly in the Scriptures, and I find in them no high praise that was just off-the-cuff. On the contrary, it seems to have been worked over and worked over.

Psalm 34 is a great psalm of praise. Did it just flow out of David like water? Well, we discover it's an acrostic, with the Hebrew alphabet built into the first letter of each line. The Spirit of God inspired it, of course—but maybe it also took David a lot of work to write it.

In fact, why shouldn't God be pleased when we work very hard to worship Him the best we can?

36

One of the great revivals of the Bible took place when the Israelites under Nehemiah rebuilt the wall of Jerusalem. The dedication of the wall became one of the spiritual high points of Jewish history. Was it spontaneous? Not on your life.

Nehemiah divided the people in half and walked them in two long lines in opposite directions along the top of the wall. They gave thanks as they walked around, accompanied by trumpeters specifically named. When the two lines met at the Prison Gate, they then proceeded together to the Temple. The singers, also named, sang loudly and clearly under the direction of Jezrahiah the choir master. You just bet they practiced!

But how lovely when worship sometimes has a spontaneous *feel*. Our own congregation loves it when sometimes we don't print an order of worship in the bulletin at all, and appear to "hang loose." We may sing unaccompanied, or one of the ministers may break into singing something familiar and everyone picks it up. . . . It appears spontaneous, but frankly, it's harder work. It had lots of planning, lots of prayer, and every participant has his own carefully timed order of service.

One thing is true; the more filled up with God the people are, the less prompting is needed from up front. If a people are alive with God, they feel completely frustrated if the paid staff does it all.

Whether the service is formal or informal, essentially it's a dialogue between up-front and pew. As with any sensitive conversationalist, the people who plan the service must be aware of talk-listen, initiate-respond flow back and forth. Of course they normally carry the heavy end—but is the whole service a monologue? If so, the people could have stayed home and gone to church via television.

Blessed black churches! When the people are exclaiming, "Yes!" "That's right!" "Amen!" at the end of every sentence in the sermon, they sure can't be going to sleep or mentally preparing the Sunday dinner.

The general rule, up-fronters, is to prepare and prepare and prepare. Think where your people are, how you can lift them to God. Plan and pray through the service to the last eyelash, with each participant ready and clued in to each other.

But then if God wants to take over and make any changes, that's up to Him.

15

THE PRE-HUDDLE HUDDLE
Pray freshness
and life into your service.

Now, if this precious bracket of Sunday time is really going to become something, the preaching minister, the minister of music, the organist, and all other key people are going to have to huddle before the play.

Say on Tuesday, after the pastor's day off. What's he preaching about next Sunday? (He told the minister of music last month, so the choir's been practicing the right anthem.) What's going to be the point of the whole service? How do you put together the parts to get across the point? What hymns, what organ music? Hey, what about so-and-so Scripture inserted, to underline the thought? Good. . . . A related solo number pops into your heads: could someone sing it right after the Scripture?

How can you involve the people to participate? (Their reading printed prayers or liturgies might be okay twice a year, but we're not trying to make robots.)*

---

* Maybe I'm wrong. Dr. Paul Rees told Ray and me that he heard a Church of England rector insist that God loves to be read to!

How can you begin the service fresh? The pastor has been <u>reading a call</u> to worship lately. Instead, maybe <u>the choir should sing</u> Paul Sjolund's thundering "O Most High, Almighty God," with full organ. Or maybe all <u>the people should sing</u> unaccompanied, "Turn Your Eyes upon Jesus."

You've been singing the Doxology to "Old Hundredth" tune for an old hundredth. Why don't you sing it to "Lasst Uns Erfrauen"?*

How can you end in a fresh way? Maybe, following the benediction, have everyone sing full voice the last phrase of Mallotte's "The Lord's Prayer": "For Thine is the kingdom and the power and the glory forever, amen!"

Every Tuesday, a huddle of up-fronters pray and rethink.

Watch it! Don't make them dizzy with too many innovations all at once. But God knows, most of us have long been dull from too few.

---

* That's "All Creatures of Our God and King."

16

THE SUNDAY MORNING HUDDLE
Unity in the Spirit
begins with the up-fronters.

Sunday School starts at 9:30, right? Or your early worship service does, perhaps.

Eight-thirty, then, should be about right for the final huddle. You're saying you went through it all last Tuesday, and the bulletin's printed, so everything's in cement?

But that's only cold paper, and now it's got to get into the hearts of everybody who's going to help it happen.

It's time for the priests to kindle the fire on the altar! It's time to pray it in, work it up! Besides, maybe God's Spirit has some last-minute change or insertion which will lift, or delightfully surprise, or add meaning.

So the minister calls the up-fronters together into his study, who are involved in the service on this particular morning. This time, for instance, it might be:

1. Harry, the minister of music;
2. Gordon, the organist;
3. Grace, who's going to sing a solo;
4. the Pastor Emeritus, who's been asked to give the morning prayer; and
5. Leo, a layman who's reading the Bible lesson.

The pastor moderates and gives a run-through of the service, item by item, with the thinking behind it. He encourages the team of the morning to make suggestions.

Harry says it would stress the meaning of the anthem's words to introduce it with one verse of Scripture. Is the team in consensus? So be it.

Gordon suggests maybe the solo should be shifted to follow the pastor's sermon.* But the closing hymn wraps it up better so that idea is tactfully shelved.

The timing is checked—got to keep the announcements bare-bones.

Then maybe 15 minutes for prayer. Each part of the service is prayed for: *Lord, just wrap them up in this morning's theme of Your forgiving love. . . . Father, cause the reading of Psalm 32:1-6 to come alive. . . .*

Each participant is prayed for: *God bless our pastor as he preaches. . . . Fill each usher with a spirit of helpfulness. . . . Quickly "settle in" the latecomers. . . . If it's Your will, don't let a baby cry! . . . Keep us from mistakes, so the concentration can be on You. . . .*

Now you're ready. (It's been a great education for Leo, and through the months many other lay people will be exposed to the philosophy of the whole service.)

But then there's Grace. She's a doll and she can really sing, but actually, she's never given any indication of spiritual life.

Suddenly, the huddle will have taught you that you can't be a mixed priesthood. You can't put strange fire

42

on the altar! From now on, the morning team will have to be solidly united in Jesus.

Then the service will start to be together.

---

* It gives a sense of beautiful flexibility to depart from the printed bulletin occasionally, when you see a better way.

17

**AND NOW,
A WORD TO THE USHERS
There are nine verses in Scripture
just for you.**

How important you are! If you're impeccably groomed, smell sweet, do your job pleasantly but modestly, and are spiritually sensitive—oh, what a difference to the whole service!

Of course you're prompt to begin your duties. Of course you encourage your fellow ushers with a smile and a handshake. Of course you smile at all comers and seat them courteously. Of course you usher almost in silence. A big grin and a whisper! That's you. They can read your lips.

But beyond those things, have you thought of these fine points? The farther forward you are in the sanctuary, the more you must keep your body movements to a minimum. During prayers, Scripture readings, musical numbers or speaking, stand still. Check discreetly with your eyes for vacant seats, but don't move; you'll distract. And of course—politely, gently, don't let anyone else move!

Wonderful if your head usher encourages you to seat latecomers at certain times, and also only in certain places—in the back, or in the balcony—so they won't break attention.

And then, that beautiful section from James 2:1-9, the ushers' portion—is just for you. It says to never fawn. Never discriminate. No play-ups, no put-downs.

Think of it: Philippians 2 says that for our sakes Jesus "made Himself of no reputation." The Greek work is *kenosis:* He divested Himself; He took off his royal robe. When He came from heaven to earth, as Lightfoot says, "He stripped Himself of the insignia of majesty."

And that, ushers, is the way all those dear people are before Him. Their clothing means nothing. Don't see pearls or furs. Don't see patches or holes. He doesn't. See precious people—in Christ, or needing Him. *"Receive them,"* says Romans 15:7. Or as *The Living Bible* puts it, "Warmly welcome each other into the church, just as Christ has warmly welcomed you."

18

IN THE HOLY OF HOLIES
A suggested running conversation with God,
as you're on your way into church.

Lord, it's a gray morning, but right now put some sunshine in my heart. We're walking into church, God: Lucy, Mark and I. Turn them on to You, Father, and do the same for me. Thank You that they're not saying anything right now so I can talk to You.

Good morning, Mrs. McGillicutty. God, she's hardly my type, but teach me to love her this morning. Do good things for her in church, too.

Morning, Elmer. Lord, thanks for Elmer. Thanks for the other ushers, too.

Father, where do we sit today? Put us strategically where we'll bless people around us. Thanks, Lord, for heading Lucy down front. What a good wife.

Lord, the murmuring seems louder than usual. Forgive us all. Please, figuratively, Lord, turn down my hearing aid.

Oh, it's so good to slide into this seat. I bow before You. You're here! You've been with me all along—praise You for that—but it's special to meet You here together with the Body.

What part of Yourself will You show today, Lord? You're exciting. Sometimes You show us Your tenderness, Your "still, small voice"—sometimes You thunder. You know my need. I'm ready.

O great God of the heavens! You are matchless. "O could I speak the matchless worth. . . ." You are worthy. You are glorious. I've used those adjectives too often, Lord. Teach me some new ones. Make me inventive in praising You.

I forgot to polish Mark's shoes. What was I doing last night that I didn't polish shoes? Oops, that's what I get for peeking. Father, forgive, shut my eyes, refocus my attention. . . .

19

THE BURDEN OF THE ORGANIST
Waiting for the sermon
to make it happen is too late.

How do people connect with God?

No doubt about it, it's mystery and miracle.

I guess we all realize, that in the majority of churches, most people only get connected to people.

No wonder most congregations are judgmental! "God's way off in heaven, but *George* is in the pulpit, and that George—ugh. . . ."

And then there's you, the organist. If your church is a people-with-people situation, then you're there for them to *review.* You're too loud, too soft, too fast, too slow, too fancy, too plain or you're just not quite on this morning.

But if you can bring them to God. . . . *IF!*

Here, like Job, I want to put my hand over my mouth. Who am I, even to offer suggestions?

Well, I confess personally much failure and a little success; but the little success I've known has been so tremendous it's worth humping and scratching and clawing for!

My organist friend, whether you're superbly trained or barely adequate, you can bring them to God, IF—

1. IF you're with Him first yourself. If you're in fellowship with Him because you've been personally cleansed by that New Testament Lamb, Jesus Christ.

2. And IF you're in fellowship with the others, too, united in heart in your common spiritual redemption and united in heart because, as in a good marriage, you're guarding your fellowship and working at it.*

3. And IF the *Word of God* is in your music—yes, it can be there—so that your keyboards communicate His specific message.

You have it in 2 Chronicles 5:11-14:

1. Verse 11 says the priests had undergone their own personal purification rites. (Man, this means *weekly!* This doesn't just mean you were saved twenty-five years ago.)

2. Verse 13 says the instrumentalists were united as one with the singers and others. (Do you need to apologize to Harry before the Sunday service?)

3. Verse 13 also gives the message of their music *in words:* they praised and thanked the Lord with, "He is so good! His lovingkindness lasts forever!"

Verse 14 gives the result: the glory of the Lord came into the Temple in brightness and power.

Still, any one-two-three formula is too pat. Enlist anybody and everybody to pray for you. Don't be too proud to ask! Will some faithful prayer warriors pray in the deacons' room straight through the service as it happens?

* You say you don't think the other up-fronters have experienced Christ's salvation? Are you sure this is the right organ job for you?

Will two in the congregation be praying for you every time you play? Will you seek to purify your own life continually so that your whole personality communicates God to them?

God isn't really being coy and playing hard to get. He wants to come among His people in reality and renewing.

A young woman in our congregation had just lost her job and she came into the sanctuary completely bewildered and discouraged.

That morning the organist happened to be playing, "Be Still, My Soul," *Finlandia* tune:

> ". . . The Lord is on thy side!
> Bear patiently the cross of grief or pain;
> Leave to thy God to order and provide—
> In every change He faithful will remain."

As on the Damascus road, God in that moment confronted her in the way. She told the congregation later that those words, like the brightness of the noonday sun, made her fall on her face and say, "Lord, what wilt Thou have me to do?"

It was the moment of a new start in her life.

20

THE PRELUDE
**It isn't supposed to come off
like restaurant dinner music.**

You're the organist at First Church and it's prelude
time. You slide onto the bench. The voices are already
raucous and rising. Two portly men are standing in the
front of the sanctuary, before everybody, guffawing over
something together. A junior high boy pounds down the
side aisle.

*O God, we're going to connect these people with You?
You're kidding! This is the opener of a high school basket-
ball game. It's got everything but popcorn and peanuts.*

And then there are my critical insides. (Mrs. McGillicutty is now standing up to wave at the ladies she saved
seats for.) *Lord, how are You going to connect my insides
with You?*

A prelude isn't supposed to come off like restaurant
dinner music. It's background, all right, but it's background to silence not background to noise.*

---

* I admit most preludes aren't background to silence. A lady told an organist
friend of mine, "Young man, your preludes are so loud, I can't hear what
my friends are saying!"

You're on your bench and you have this dream: your music is going to hush them, lead them to silence, then to worship. You're going to start connecting them with God.

How?

1. About the volume. Years ago my first attempts to quiet the people were demonic. I'd work up to a huge climax and cut off. . . . Let Mrs. McGillicutty find herself screaming in church and maybe she'd be embarrassed enough to quit.

Actually, though, variety in volume is crucial. It will cut down the talking. Work up, work down. Be suddenly soft. (Forget the suddenly loud.) Sometimes pause altogether between numbers.

2. Enlist the minister's help. He can come in before your prelude, or at a stopping place during it, and speak to the people about the need for silence, for heart preparation, about the purpose of the prelude; and he can ask them to find their seats quickly and get right to God, et cetera. Just a few sentences each Sunday—maybe 60 seconds' worth—will start paying off.

Then he can sit bowed in prayer and set an example!

3. Do you know the power of a hymn? Brother, between those two hard covers in your hands, you've got dynamite. Play your classical repertoire, of course—as lofty and intricate as your skill allows—but for connecting people with God, HYMNS ARE WHERE THE POWER CONNECTS.

21

HYMNS ARE WHERE
THE POWER CONNECTS
**The "flesh" of music becomes Word—
and we behold His glory!**

Read 1 Corinthians 14:2-12 to see that worshipers have got to understand what's going on. Organist, if your preludes and offertories are always classical unknowns how are your people going to get the message? The apostle Paul talks about flutes and trumpets, and says if they don't play a clear melody, where's the communication?

Let's focus in, now.

How do you communicate? *How can the notes you play do anything to the hearts of your people?*

All right, so you're going to try hymns for part of the prelude time. Don't just flip the hymnbook pages and start in. No, no! TO CONNECT YOUR PEOPLE WITH GOD takes strategy—all the strategy you can scratch, claw, and dig for.

You know your people. Pick out hymns they know the words to (at least one verse). And pick hymns whose subjects make sense when you put them together. Gradually they'll get the purpose behind your playing. They'll start to THINK as they listen.

What subjects? Intensely personal ones. Out of your playing, you want WORDS to pop into their heads:

"My God, how wonderful Thou art! . . ."

"Nearer, still nearer. . . ."

If your music is to be the background to what they're doing, you want to give powerful suggestions so they'll *do the right thing*. (Not to find out how Uncle John's gallbladder is this week, but to get quickly, individually, to the Person of God.)

"I need Thee, O I need Thee! . . ."

Get through to them—oh, get through! This breakthrough of your spiritual message into their consciousness can be the most important key to their mentally turning off each other and turning on to Christ. That's why key, familiar phrases must be strongly fervent.

(Organist to people: "I believe this with all my heart. I'm playing it this way so you'll get it and believe it too!")

Remember, you're not edifying yourself. Use what blesses *them*. Pull some hymns from the memories of the old-timers, some that are contemporary. (Easy does it; wrap it all up in tenderness and dignity.) Catch the ears of the little ones: "Praise Him, Praise Him, All Ye Little Children" will speak to the tiniest tot—and his grandfather.

Be sure to give plenty of variety in volume. What a trap we've fallen into lately, thinking "worshipful" meant "quiet"! How inhibited we've become, how insipid our church services! Can you believe it—when Nehemiah led the people in worship the joy of Jerusalem was heard in all the surrounding country!* Sometimes worship is loud: "Shout for joy, all ye peoples!" (God, You're so great!) Sometimes worship is quiet: "Be still, and know that I am God." (I wait before You, Lord.)

Organist friend, ring the changes! "How do I love Thee, God? Let me count the ways. . . ."

* Nehemiah 12:43.

22

PLAIN OR FANCY?
There are always those musicians
who feel that hymns are beneath them. . . .

A hymn is like a woman. Her intrinsic beauty and
worth are absolutely established. But you can sure dress
her up or down according to the occasion.

Hymns in church? Sometimes up, sometimes down.

If a choir has sung a number of anthem-type hymn
arrangements lately, it's probably time to sing one right
out of the hymnbook—one that touches the heart, straight
and sincere. Your people will hum it the whole next
week.

An organist can lift new beauty out of old hymns
by using many of the stunning hymn arrangements on
the market today—arrangements which still bring out the
melody line so that the message is clearly there. But
maybe another time he'll play, "Jesus Loves Me, This
I Know" simply, genuinely, one chord at a time and
no passing tones.

Organist, are you gifted in arranging? Then shelve old Bach for a while, and do exactly what he did in his day for his congregation: take your people's current favorite hymn tunes, make the melodies stand out strong and clear, and give them backgrounds as patterned as old lace.

One warning, though. Too many embellished hymns are like too many fat people all in one room. You begin to long for a little bony structure to show; you begin to try to think what the original is really like underneath.

Singers and players, do you know what will make your hymns most beautiful? Live right, friends; live right.

23

SUGGESTIONS
FOR NON-CREATIVE ORGANISTS
And for other organists who go dry.
I'm going to keep this book around;
I'll be needing it.

Organist, you're preparing for Sunday's prelude.

Suppose this Sunday you want to encourage people to meditate on God's leadership. You could:

1. Start with, "Lead On, O King Eternal," melody line only with a solo trumpet stop. (Catch the ear of Mrs. McGillicutty.)

2. Move on to, "He Leadeth Me"; "Guide Me, O Thou Great Jehovah"; "Lead, Kindly Light"; "Where He Leads Me"; "O Master, Let Me Walk with Thee." For the old-timers, "Footprints of Jesus"; for the teenagers, "I Have Decided to Follow Jesus."

Just use the ones *your* church people really know and respond to.

Or suppose you'd like them to meditate on the quiet of God.

1. Do they know, "The Lord Is in His Holy Temple"? Do it high on one manual, no pedals. "Let all the earth keep silence before Him. . . ."

2. Then maybe, "Dear Lord and Father of Mankind," with a pretty 16′ stop. "Forgive our feverish ways. . . ." (The Jones family have just settled into their pew after an hour's nightmare of spilled cornflakes and lost socks.)

3. How about, "Near to the Heart of God": "There is a place of quiet rest . . ." and use some chimes.

Or you want "praise" for your theme. What a subject! And so much to choose from.

1. No tremolo—maybe, "All People That on Earth Do Dwell," Old Hundredth in its original rhythm, crisp and attention getting.

2. No pause, straight into, "When Morning Gilds the Skies," light but bright! Repeat it, bigger and bigger—

3. Suddenly soft, into, "Praise Him, Praise Him, All Ye Little Children." Why not?

4. Maybe, "Hallelujah! What a Saviour!"—the chorus of, "Our Great Saviour," Hyfrydol tune—

5. Then, "O Could I Speak the Matchless Worth"—build it to a finish of fanfare and thunder.

How many subjects can you minister to them about? You'll never run out. Many subjects are obvious, from your hymnal's Topical Index. Put together, "Near to the Heart of God"; "Nearer, Still Nearer"; "Nearer, My God, to Thee"; "O For a Closer Walk."

Put together, "All Hail the Power of Jesus' Name"; "The Name of Jesus"; "How Sweet the Name of Jesus Sounds"; the chorus of, "He Keeps Me Singing"; "Take the Name of Jesus with You."

Put together, "Holy Bible, Book Divine"; "Thy Word

Is Like a Garden, Lord"; "Break Thou the Bread of Life"; "Open My Eyes, That I May See"; "More About Jesus."

Put together, "Holy Ghost, with Light Divine"; "Breathe on Me, Breath of God"; "Spirit of God, Descend upon My Heart"; "Fill Me Now."

Don't put *any* of them together unless they're meaningful to *your* congregation. Use what "turns them on."

If you're gifted at arranging, transposing, modulating—my friend, be challenged to the hilt. Put them together like a sermon, with valleys, plains, and peaks in perfect proportion; with the right "feel" as you change keys to increase the fervor or to subside. And all of it to put across the message in the most vivid way possible.

And if you can't do these things? If it's in your heart, you can still pack a wallop through hymns.

Plan your theme.

Pick out your hymns.

Arrange them in order of message, key changes, dynamics, emotion, et cetera.

Practice like crazy.

Next Sunday morning you'll be ready to prop open your pages and *tell 'em the story.*

24

WHAT HYMNS?
ALL CHURCH STAFFERS, TAKE NOTE
"After all, I've had *years* of training,
and only the best is good enough for God . . ."
signed, the Flesh.

A Communion cup is a Communion cup is a Communion cup. It is set apart from all common uses to a sacred use. Never mind if it's cleverly shaped or if the silver's wearing thin. Its use is settled; its contents bring blessing.

Whichever one you are, O Communion cup, you are beautiful because you are in Jesus' hands to be used.

A Christian is a Christian is a Christian. He is potentially perfect and full of glory; he is in heaven's eyes complete; he is beautiful. He may have warts and moles, be halt, maimed, or blind; he may be shaped like a pear or wrinkled like a prune.

O believer—whoever you are, God's heart is full of love for you and I want my heart stretched until it's full of love for you, too.

A tried-and-true hymn is a tried-and-true hymn is a tried-and-true hymn. It is no longer on trial; only my judgment of it is. It may be trite, it may be emotional, it may be (horrors!) subjective instead of objective. . . .

O lowliest, poorest little hymn, I bow my head and acknowledge that you probably have brought more blessing to the church than I personally ever will. Forgive my judgmental spirit. I may not use you, but I will rejoice when others do. The members of the Body are varied but all precious; their hymns are varied but all precious, too. Forgive my student-day snickers. I've put away childish things.

The theme of the morning's service is God's love. The opening hymn is "Love Divine, All Love Excelling"; the minister is going to read the last soaring verses of the eighth chapter of Romans; why shouldn't the organist play for the offertory, "Jesus Loves Even Me"?

The choir anthem this particular Sunday is contemporary and dissonant and loud! It's great—exciting—but a few white-haired saints may experience a little future shock. God bless them, they won't be around forever to be ministered to. Pastor, let them read or recite the Twenty-third Psalm. Organist, play for them, "Tell Me the Story of Jesus," or "In the Sweet By and By," or "Rock of Ages."

This isn't politicking. It's being sensitive to all the flock and bringing a balanced diet to the service.

It may even keep Mrs. McGillicutty from changing her membership over to the Church of the Good Shepherd.

25

INSTEAD OF A PRELUDE
There are lots of ways
to prepare for worship.

Did you ever have your congregation enter in total silence? We did once. We had the ushers whisper the word. It was fantastic. People really prayed. Or read their Bibles. Or at least their bulletins. No doubt a few didn't get the word and thought the organist was sick, or the organ had blown a fuse.

Do you have a singing congregation? Go from favorite hymn to favorite hymn, playing just enough introduction for the people to identify it, and let them sing along—seated—on first verses only. No hymnbooks. The minister of music or any singing man can be seated up front to start them out.

Other instruments are a wonderful change. A violin, a flute, a cello, a harp—

A guitar? Well, you know your church, I don't.

26

BODY LANGUAGE
IS POWERFUL COMMUNICATION
When you're in church, how do you look?

Worshipers all have to be taught how to worship. We may have gone to church for years and yet never developed our worshiping muscles!

Let none of us assume we know how. In fact, scenes of heaven in the book of Revelation seem so foreign to us we probably know much less than we think we know.

But let's deal with the obvious.

Churchgoer, *when* do you walk in the door? Henrietta Mears used to say, "If you're not ten minutes early, you're late!"

The idea is to express eagerness. If you stand around yakking outside, you give off the aroma that you consider meeting people more important than meeting God. If you rush up in your car at the last minute, you give the impression that you consider bed more important.

How do you walk in the door? Come in meekly from the back entrance. (From the front you distract.) Tiptoe in, *sneak* in. Assume that of course everyone seated is already seeking to connect with God. Greet the usher with a smile and a whisper.

Now, using as little motion as possible, go all the way to the front row if you're first—or fill in immediately behind. That way your body is going to set the pattern for worshipful behavior behind you and you won't be disturbed by those who come after you.

Body language! Oh, what it does for the Body! Slide into your seat, shut out those around you and bow very low in obvious, earnest prayer. Talk about it all to God and don't hurry. Confess your sins, get clean and ready. When you've really lingered before Him then get into the Book. Not the pew Bible but your own; read, mark, pray, think, be quiet. Gorgeous!

Body language! Do you understand it? If you really understood that you were in face-to-face encounter with Jesus Christ, could you slouch back in your seat with right foot over left knee? Could you keep your head up, swiveling to look around? God help us all!

Body language! Every physical body sets the mood for the twenty or thirty people situated around and behind him. Earnestness must show! When you pray, *pray.** When you listen, *listen.* A guy can turn his head to gaze admiringly at his girl and wash worship down the drain for twenty people sitting behind him. Or he can turn his head to nod at his girl a confirmation of a point in the sermon, and behind him twenty hearts will beat faster.

Bodies talk volumes.

---

* When Hannah moved her lips, the spiritual life of her day was at such a low ebb, Eli her priest thought she was drunk. He didn't even recognize earnest praying when he saw it!

27

THE BODY OF CHRIST
NOURISHES ITSELF IN WORSHIP
Every member feeds
every other member.

What do you suppose are, say, the three most important contributions you make—to God and to each other—when you gather with other believers to worship? I'm thinking about it, and I can suggest three: total, earnest concentration; sincerity; and prayer.

Total, earnest concentration. Even a mother with wiggly kids can learn, with her eyes fixed up front and heaven on her face, to pinch! Pinching is the perfect discipline for church. As she becomes expert she can keep her hands positioned so that even the most alert person behind her could not possibly detect it. And she can learn the precise pressure of a pinch which will send the message without producing an overreaction.

Sincerity. Think about it. You're all singing:

"See, from His head, His hands, His feet,
Sorrow and love flow mingled down. . . ."

In the middle of the phrase some singer grins hello at a friend, and something's lost that cannot be regained.

Prayer. Christians united in worship must be taught when concentration of prayer is particularly needed. Recognize the red-flag signals: a baby begins to cry, a fire engine clangs by outside, somebody gets sick. Especially when the preacher is coming to the clincher of his sermon with an important appeal for response from the listeners—from somewhere, raucous kids are released from Sunday School.

The magnetic field of the Holy Spirit often becomes a field of battle. Learn to smell war in the air, and bear down in prayer.

Every congregation has a choice to be one of two things. You can choose to be a bag of marbles, single units that don't affect each other except in collision. On Sunday morning you can choose to go to church or to sleep in: who really cares whether there are 192 or 193 marbles in a bag?

Or you can choose to be a bag of grapes. The juices begin to mingle, and there is no way to extricate yourselves if you tried. Each is part of all. Part of the fragrance. Part of the "stuff."

28

UP-FRONTERS, YOUR BODIES MATTER, TOO
Unless you're buried behind an altar rail or in a console pit.

Interesting that most up-fronters are not only audible but also visible. Are you going to ask God to make eternity come ringing through your words and music—and then do it with wooden faces and stiff backs?

No, no.

Now, this is delicate. The difference between the externally flamboyant and theatrical and the wholly enthusiastic, body, soul, and spirit, may be a difference that is discernible only because of your life all week long; because of your asking God to make you come across in sincerity; and because of the whole atmosphere of a prayer-backed service.

When Ray was in preaching class at Princeton, his prof wouldn't let the students preach standing back on their heels. In that stance, they didn't care much about what they were saying. They had to preach leaning forward, standing on the balls of their feet. Body language! *I care. I love you. I believe this. Dear flock, listen.*

Organist, when you play, sing. For one thing, your own singing and breathing will be a check on the tempo. But more, you're together, you're part of them. *This is not just an organ job to me. I'm praising, too; I'm asking Him, too; I'm doing what you're doing; I'm with you in this, dear people.*

Organist, if you must change stops during a prayer, do it quickly, then tune your heart to God. Or don't set up the registration for your next cue and then blank out. Listen to everything!

Minister of music, is there a responsive reading? You read, too. And let your face be part of all the action. Rejoice with those who rejoice, and weep with those who weep. Grapes in the bag together!

All up-fronters, when the sermon time comes, don't you dare walk out—not even if you have three consecutive services. (How will the people know you don't go out for coffee all three times? It hurts morale.) Give the preaching all your attention, no matter how many times you've heard it. Use your Bible. Take notes. Pray for the preacher.

How God must love those of His children who are faithfully involved in preaching or playing or singing for three or four services every Sunday! What a precious, special breed they are: they with the slightly numb backsides, and serious attention on their beautiful faces.

29

**HOW TO SING
A CONGREGATIONAL HYMN
In one easy lesson.**

Sing!*

---

* One preacher once stopped a hymn in the middle and cried out in desperation,
"If you people don't sing, I can't preach!"

30 *Ideas*

ORGAN BRIDGES
Don't just diddle around.

The first congregational hymn is over, the amen has been sung, everybody's sitting down, and the organist is supposed to keep playing for a moment while ushers seat latecomers.

Right?

This is the great moment of truth—the great exposure of the organist's personal religion.

Did I overstate? Well, it's the great reflection of the organist's personal opinion of the worship service.

Organist, don't just diddle around.

Say something!

Has the congregation just sung, "O Worship the King"? Continue full organ with, "Come, Thou Almighty King," and pray He'll come.

They've just sung, "O Worship the King" and now the pastor is going to pray? Well, then, back down and bridge into,

> "King of my life, I crown Thee now;
> Thine shall the glory be. . . ."

Maybe the pastor would begin his prayer on the "King" theme.

Or they've just sung, "Praise Ye the Lord, the Almighty" or "The God of Abraham Praise." Something big! How about straight into the chorus of, "To God Be the Glory. . . . Praise the Lord, praise the Lord, Let the earth hear His voice!"

Romans 12 says to be fervent in spirit. That includes church organists as they play bridges after opening hymns. Don't sound like a prayer response. Get underneath it and urge it along. Play it with heart!

It was the first Sunday in December at Lake Avenue Church. Advent Season!

The opening hymn was, "O Come, O Come, Emmanuel." The organ followed by bridging into the old children's chorus, "Into My Heart." ("Come into my heart, Lord Jesus. . . .")

Immediately, two pastors read Psalm 24 antiphonally:

"Open up, O ancient gates, and let the King of Glory in."

"Who is this King of Glory?"

"The Lord, strong and mighty, invincible in battle. Yes, open wide the gates and let the King of Glory in!"

"Who is this King of Glory?"
"The Lord of Hosts: He is the King of Glory!"
Without a pause a tenor soloist began to sing,

"Thou didst leave Thy throne and Thy kingly crown
When Thou camest to earth for me;
But in Bethlehem's home was there found no room
For Thy holy nativity:
O come to my heart, Lord Jesus!
There is room in my heart for Thee!"

The organ followed a half step higher in key with
an urgent repetition,

"Into my heart, into my heart,
Come into my heart, Lord Jesus. . . ."

There was a real sense of prayerful expectancy over
the people for His very special presence.

And He was there.

31

ABOUT THE SPECIAL MUSIC
If any.

No, there isn't any value in adding to an up-front performance just in the spirit of, "The Show Must Go On."

Minister of music, why should you arrange for "special music," anthems, solos, duets, instrumental numbers, and so on? Because the more ways in which we can get the members of the Body to "talk" to one another, the better. They need to communicate, participate, testify, praise, exhort, encourage—everything; and if the Spirit has gifted them to do it through music, that's part of the participation.

Then the music becomes *real.*

Believers communicate with believers, and the vehicle is music. (Occasionally it might be believers communicate with unbelievers, urging them to come to Christ.)

Then how will you choose the music that is special? Well, you see what's going on in that particular service: what the pastor's preaching about, if missionaries are being welcomed home, or a new Christian is giving a testimony, or it's "youth emphasis" Sunday, or whatever—and you build on that.

So the whole service will then become a piece.

Of course you'll look for variety of presentation: a big, ornate choir number; a simple, childlike hymn for the choir to sing; a duet, a flute, a mixed quartet, a violin. . . .

But first you look for *heart* in the performers. Then you choose the musical message that will fit the performers' spiritual experience as well as fit the need of the morning.

Where do these come from?

From God the Spirit.

Then how do you find "special music"?

Ask Him.

32

THE PASTORAL PRAYER
It's a demonstration
of a representative form of government.

When a congregation is together in worship, any prayers ought to be total-participation situations. We don't have the right to waste the saints' precious time with anything less than that which involves everybody.

This gives congregational prayer a choice of these forms, among others:

1. *Silent prayer.* Let it be really silent! We can't concentrate on talking to Him against background music. Subjects for praying may be suggested by the minister in brief, occasional words.

2. *Audible, spontaneous prayer by all simultaneously.* Some Christian groups around the world always pray this way; most never do. It can be stimulating and refreshing.

3. *Audible prayers read in unison from a prayer book or bulletin.* Perhaps the best rule here is, if you *always* do it, consider quitting for awhile; if you *never* do it, consider doing it occasionally.

4. *Voluntary "sentence prayers" on behalf of all.* Our own church people enjoy this, even with a thousand people together. The rules are: speak up so all can hear, and pray only one or two sentences. Often we participate on a specific theme of praise or petition.

5. *Several laymen designated in advance to pray on behalf of all.* These can stand and pray in turn from their pews or they can come together at the pulpit first and take turns there. How precious this method has been for us overseas in multi-language situations, when godly laymen prayed, each in his own tongue, on behalf of various segments of the people!

6. *One pastor in the pulpit praying on behalf of all.* Variations of this are several pastors in the pulpit—or a pastor and a layman—praying conversationally back and forth on behalf of their people.

Again, it must be stressed that this is representational praying! It is on behalf of the whole Body. No pastor has the right to pray, "Lord, forgive us for communicating poorly with each other" because Deacon Charlie Jones forgot to tell him about a business item, and he hopes Charlie will get the point and get with it. Neither is it Sneaky Announcement Time: "Lord, bless the Shnooker family whose aunt died last Thursday," or "Lord, bless the Sunday School picnic coming up this Friday afternoon at five. . . . Bless all those who bring an extra dozen cookies. . . . Help them to remember it will be held in the high school gym in case of rain. . . ."

No, this prayer is *on behalf of all the family of God,* praying in their stead to Him.

We get the picture from 1 Kings 8 and 2 Chronicles 6, King Solomon's prayer on behalf of all his people.

His posture varied. He was up on a platform out of doors; sometimes he faced the Temple; sometimes he faced the people; sometimes he stood, sometimes he knelt down before them, reaching his arms toward heaven.

His subject matter was consistent: he referred 94 times to God, 81 times to the people of God. His prayer was to relate them to each other.

It was all carefully planned. It had symmetry and form: an invocation, a blessing, a time of petition, another blessing. It concerned God's glory, sin, trouble, obedience, disobedience, God's promises, God's forgiveness, the people's spiritual history—it had lofty themes, majestic scope! How lifting; how realistic, but how stretching congregation-wide prayers should be!

And what a part we people in the pew must play! If that one who prays represents *me,* I must be continually echoing an amen in my heart: "That's right, Father. . . . Yes, do it. . . . I agree to what he's saying. . . ." My listening must be in active, aggressive partnership.

Variations in posture? Wouldn't it be glorious if we were free enough of our inhibitions to stand, sit, or kneel as our individual hearts required, lifting arms or not, eyes closed to all around, but ears and hearts opened to heaven?!

As Solomon finished his prayer in 2 Chronicles 7:1, fire came out of heaven and all the people fell flat on the pavement.

Words fail me.

33

THE OFFERTORY
Oops,
Mrs. McGillicutty is at it again.

The prelude and the offertory are the two points in many a service that signal Happy Talk Time.

They also are the two points when usually nothing's doing except the organ.

Organist, does that tell you something?*

* Everything that was said in chapters 19-25 and 35, 39 applies here.

34

WHY AM I WRITING?
WHY ARE YOU READING?
Let's stop a minute
and check motives.

All this can't be a self-improvement course. Or church-improvement course.

Father, if I'm writing this to become an "author," forget the whole thing. Settle me back to rest anonymously and contentedly in Your love.

Lord, if these readers are reading to become "Super-Worshipers". . . .

(*"None of the other churches in our town know how to worship, but boy, do we. . . ."*

"All the rest of these people sitting around me in church are just aware of one another, but I'm aware of God. . . ."

"If we can just latch onto some of these exciting techniques we can lure all the saints out of the church-up-the-street and into our church. . . .")

God, we're unprofitable servants. May the hot flames of Your purifying judgment sizzle and crackle within us until ego is but gray ash, wafting impotently away.

Lord, this is all for You. This is to give You pleasure. This is to make You delighted with us. . . .!

35

CHURCH PEOPLE, GET WITH IT!
If you sing, *sing.*
If you play, *play.* If you preach, *preach.*

There is nothing so important in religion as whole-heartedness.

The Psalmist said, "With my whole being will I praise Thee!"* "Forever and forever I will sing about the tender mercies of the Lord!"**

If I were a betting person, I'd bet the worst malady of church people everywhere isn't poor taste or singing sour notes; it's lack of conviction.

Friends, do what you do with intensity. This doesn't necessarily mean being garish or sensational or loud. It simply means that whatever you do you communicate—audibly and visibly—to God and to one another. So do only what is meaningful; eliminate all else from worship; and then what you do, do with all your heart.

Think of the emotion built into our hymns:

"Thou, O Christ, art all I want;
   More than all in Thee I find. . . ."

"O joy that seekest me through pain, . . .
   I cannot close my heart to thee."

* Psalm 9:1
** Psalm 89:1

81

"The dearest idol that I have known,
Whate'er that idol be,
Help me to tear it from Thy throne
And worship only Thee!"

"That soul, though all hell
Should endeavor to shake,
I'll never, no, never,
No, never forsake!"

"Jesus, Thy blood and righteousness
My beauty are, my glorious dress.
'Midst flaming worlds, in these arrayed,
With joy shall I lift up my head!"

Joy, glory, hallelujah! What excitement! How dare we play or sing a message, such as this, like weak tea and toast?

Take another example:

"Face to face with Christ, my Saviour—"

We can't sing and play it full of cream puffs and marshmallows.

Face to face—just Him and me?

My God, I'll never sing it or play it again until You teach me how to communicate it.

36

CLASSICAL ORGAN LITERATURE
HAS ITS PLACE
If you keep it in its place.

Praise God for all the beauty He's inspired in this world! Praise Him for the proportions of arches and columns and spires in St. Stephen's Church in Vienna! Praise Him for the colors that glow from the windows of Canterbury Cathedral in south England! Praise Him for so-called "secular" beauty, too: the architecture of Lima, the flower beds of Tivoli!

When God made us in His image, one manifestation of that is that we are busy little "creators." Look down from any airplane and marvel at it.

So praise God for every piece of good, classical music; yes, and praise God *with* it, too—IF, IF, IF! It must have a spirit about it that makes it fit. It must be very special if it's to be drafted for God's service. The world is full of secular music situations. Most secular music should stay right there.

And sacred music in your church? Well, it depends on *which piece.* Would you want any ordained minister in the world to preach in your pulpit? Then neither does all sacred music fit your church. An "Ave Maria" at First Methodist would be a little grotesque.

But more: a prelude or choir anthem that's right for a college campus church may be all wrong for a rural community. Where are your people? Respect them, honor them, and *meet them where they are.*

Yes, many voices will clamor, "But church music—and sermons, too—should also lift and educate." May I gently suggest that a leader has to be out in front *a little way,* but not too far. If the gap's too wide, they'll never follow him.

And anyway, sniff the aroma of that "education" comment. Was that a haughty spirit talking? Maybe the church musician or the preacher needs to learn more from their people in certain areas than the people need to learn about music or theology. Listen to your dear flock. Get to know them deeply, their needs, their joys. Then lift and educate and make them what they could never have been without your ministry.

But also,—*scratch 'em where they itch.*

So how do you pick what you're going to play, organist? Well, here's the point: never play a single note without meaning.

Never!

To the extent that you put in filler which is excelsior and sawdust, to that extent your people will be tempted to grow dull and ho-hum as you play.

Even a wordless classical number must create the spirit of connecting the people with God—or else forget it

Maybe you'll do it through George Bohm's "Lord Jesus Christ, Be Present Now" (meditative, pre-Bach). Maybe you'll do it through Sigfried Kerg-Elert's "Lord Jesus Christ, Be Present Now" (big, ornate, twentieth century).

And, oh, there's a rich wealth of organ literature to use! Search constantly to find the treasures, those pieces through which the spiritual heart of the composer glows—pieces that will beautify and heighten the effect of the service.

But if the piece isn't doing the job, shelve it.

Be honest: are you ever tempted to show off? Walk out the door and go get a cup of coffee. Hassle it out with God and don't come back to your work until self is put down and you're ready to minister—only minister.

Only minister?

Ministering is absolutely the most!

Lord, what can we do next Sunday that will break into glory?

37

ESSENTIAL INGREDIENTS
FOR A HAPPENING

We were sitting in a little theater in Disneyland, watching an old film clip of Walt Disney philosophizing on what makes a good movie. Back he leaned in his leather chair.

"Nobody could have predicted how well 'Snow White' was going to do," he said. "Not in our wildest dreams. Heady with success, we put together another, 'Alice in Wonderland.' But do you know—it never went over very well.

"So we sat back and tried to analyze why. And we came to the conclusion that 'Snow White'—and every successful production—had two ingredients: laughter and tears.

"That was a milestone discovery," said Mr. Disney, in his modest, chatty way. "After that, everything we turned out had to have both laughter and tears. . . ."

Ray and I grabbed that one. Every conference we speak at must have laughter and tears. Every speaking date, every worship service. At least we can aim for it, have it in mind, ask God for it. A happening—a real, to-be-remembered occasion—needs truth (doctrine—thoughtful, nitty-gritty substance), but it also needs to be clothed in laughter and tears.

In the deep jungles of Peru in December of 1972, we were with Wycliffe missionaries when God met them in a fresh way. Some of those strong men wept so hard before their brothers they were literally supported by friends who came and stood with them as they spoke. And yet God the Spirit knew they couldn't have stood tears without laughter: just as one dear woman was ready to testify, a bug crawled down her dress. . . . For lack of tissue in jungle conditions, they wept into yards of toilet paper, and even that broke them up. . . .

Tears and laughter can't be contrived. You're on the lookout for them—but mostly, you ask God to make them happen.

And me in a church pew? If something strikes me funny, or if tears well up in my throat, I welcome both as friends. "Hey—the Holy Spirit is here, doing something. Praise God. Keep coming on, Father."

Look for them—in the pulpit, in the pew—those wonderful little extra touches from heaven, laughter and tears.

38

ARE YOUR CHOIR MEMBERS
REALLY ALL THERE IN WORSHIP?
Or is it for them
a moonlighting job?

You've come through the first half of your church service: the hymns have been sung, the offering's been taken, and the minister is going to preach. Then, every Sunday like clockwork, there's a stealthy exodus—in front of the whole congregation. All those black-robed choir members vanish out a side door.

You whisper to the first-time visitor sitting beside you, "They're going out to attend Sunday School this hour. Some of them teach classes." Or are they going out for breakfast? Or home to bed? And were they *really* in church all through the other service, or aren't they hearing the pastor's sermon at all? You have an uncomfortable sense of maybe being cheated on.

Do you remember that the Israelite singers were full-time? It was all they did, as service to God. Now, I know that many choir members feel a legitimate need for getting in on Sunday School as well—but maybe others need to be challenged to be a "core choir" that stays straight through both (or maybe two out of three) morning services. Then other choir members will add to them for one hour and be in Sunday School the other—but when they're there, they're there for the entire service.

Do you know how beautiful it is, not to have any exodus? And the freedom which suddenly opens up? You can put the sermon first, last, or in the middle; the choir is there to be used at any time. Praise the Lord!

It makes a gorgeous difference in the whole service in the feeling of commitment. *We are together, brothers and sisters; we are all together, and we aren't going anywhere else, because our hearts are all here to worship God for this whole hour.*

39

THE MINISTER OF MUSIC
UNDERSHEPHERDS HIS CHOIRS
He's got to be at least
as much "minister" as "music."

How can you persuade full choirs of people to give themselves to the kind of commitment necessary to do the job? Minister of music or choir director, that's got to be your burden. Prayer is going to have to surround them like a cloud. Let every choir member be a prayer partner with another choir member. In addition, let each choir member have two members of the congregation pledged to support him in prayer every time he sings. Every autumn or new semester the choir people can put quarters into a kitty until they're able to report who their prayer partners and prayer supporters are!

The point is not the mechanics of prayer. The point is that unless the Holy Spirit breathes His life into our music, all it will be is *music*. For that, we can turn on any radio.

Minister of music, are you just *music*, or do you minister? When you look at Susie Schleirmacher, whom do you see? An alto? Or do you see a wife with an overbearing husband, a new home, and an honor-student daughter? Are your people *people* (to be ministered to) or *things* (to be used)?

If at any rehearsal you face four sections of *things*, you'll trumpet, "Okay-let's-get-started-we've-got-lotsa-work-to-do-here-tonight-Thanksgiving's-coming-up-and-we-haven't-even-started-on-Christmas-and-I-wonder-if-one-of-you-low-altos-couldn't-sing-tenor?"

But if you face *people*, you'll shepherd them. First you'll take time to worship, to lift them to God. Then you may take time to make sure their hearts are okay; maybe let them share joys and burdens in twos and threes and pray for one another for a little while. When the hurts are eased and the joys expressed and they're getting more deeply involved in one another's lives—

Then begin to sing.

I want to tell you, it will make a difference in the final *sound*.

40

REBUTTAL TO, "WE DON'T HAVE TO PRACTICE, IT'S ONLY A HYMN"

For more than a decade, I've been organist for Charles E. Fuller's "Old Fashioned Revival Hour" radio program—now David Hubbard's, "The Joyful Sound."

Here's how the broadcast tapes were made:

In the studio stand thirty or so singers, many of whom earn their living in full-time professional music.

Rudy Atwood sits at the piano, a world-famous careerist loved by Christians everywhere.

Under Dr. Leland Green's hands, we'll sweat out five literal minutes on one completely familiar old line:

"Saviour, more than life to me,
I am clinging, clinging close to Thee. . . ."

Dr. Green says we're relaxing the dotted eighths and sixteenths into triplets and ruining the rhythm. We work that through. Then we synchronize all the R's at the end of "more" and the TH's of the word "than." We pull out "life" a little. We dip a little in volume after "me" without actually breathing. We do "clinging, clinging" until we ring like bells.

When all the mechanics are conquered, he says, "Now add heart." For another five minutes we work on that musical line in the dimension of His being more than life—searching for depths of sincerity by "thinking" the message as we sing or play it.

We may spend thirty minutes to put it all together as if we'd never seen it before.

Each week, Dr. Leland Green brings resurrection out from under his hands. Everyone who's been under that strict training knows that from the familiar can spring life and renewal and exciting meaning.

41

A SERVICE'S FLOW
"Now, folks—heh, heh—Susie Schleirmacher is going to favor us with an offertory solo."

You're looking at television. Some historic occasion is being brought live to you and in the middle of the screen you're supposed to see the world-famous Mr. So-and-So in the act of doing such-and-such—the most important act of this generation. Unfortunately, a twelve-year-old kid has discovered the camera's live, so there he is, out of focus, in the foreground covering the screen, waving frantically and hamming it up.

And here's church. The act on the screen is the greatest of all: God redeeming man. ("O Lord of Hosts, God of Israel enthroned above the cherubim, You alone are God of all the kingdoms of the earth. . . .")

But unfortunately, all we can see is George—hearty, folksy, grinning George, "Thank you, choir, for that fantastic number, yessir, you folks musta really practiced that one; and now everybody turn to hymn 22 and let's really hear you sing it like you mean it, yessir, that's what we're all here for, so let's just let it all out, are you ready on the first word. . . ."

The *Los Angeles Times* writer Charles Champlin says, "In art, *less is more*. What is true can always be simply said."*

"Less is more!" Job to God: "I lay my hand upon my mouth in silence. I have said too much already."

"Less is more!" Pastor, please read through the chapters in this book for your other staffers, and tell them to read your chapters. (All of you have to melt together into the same flavor!) In chapter 36 on classical organ literature there are these sentences: "Never play a single note without meaning. . . . To the extent that you put in filler which is excelsior and sawdust, to that extent your people will be tempted to grow dull and ho-hum as you play."

This is just as true of speaking. Now, perhaps God has made you a hearty and verbose person. He works through personalities so don't think you suddenly have to become Austere Arthur.

But look at your printed order of worship. There's no reason to repeat orally what's already before their eyes. If the transition needs music, let the organ bridge it meaningfully (or a soloist, or the choir, or whatever). If the need of the moment is the spoken word, don't duplicate the printed page, but supplement it. Call attention to the meaning of what's happening; let someone

* Would you agree that a worship service is man's highest art form?

else read a verse of related Scripture, or a quotation, or—

Once, just before our choir was going to sing about Christ's second coming to earth, Ray had two laymen read current newspaper headlines back and forth for about one minute—fulfillments of prophecy as a buildup to the fantastic news that He's coming!

Think about your service's flow. Your subject matter is so tremendous that maybe your biggest need is to prune and let the subject matter show!

"Less is more."

42

ANNOUNCEMENTS
Clear your brain,
here comes a new metaphor.

The worship service is a fire you're feeding. And the announcement time is a filled squirt gun.

"Next Tuesday morning the ladies will gather at ten o'clock in the parlor to quilt. . . ." Psss! One of the flames is shot out.

"If there are any volunteers to help in the Daily Vacation Bible School starting tomorrow morning, would you please see Rachel McGruder. . . ." Pow! Another part of the fire goes cold.

A few more and you may be hunting for matches again.

Announcements are the only part of a service which, by their very nature, edify nobody. They in no way build up the Body or introduce unbelievers to the Saviour. Hearts do not beat faster over announcements.

Therefore here are a few suggested rules:

1. Announcements should not repeat what is already in the bulletin. Americans are something like 97 percent literate. Announcements are what bulletins were invented for.

2. Announcements should not pertain to only a part of the congregation (a committee, the young people, the women, etc.). A worship service is a togetherness experience. Don't lessen that by excluding large segments of people, not even for 60 seconds.

Let the special groups learn to rely on the bulletin, on bulletin inserts, on posters around the church campus, on the mails, on telephones, etc. But don't let them intrude into worship.

3. Never announce appeals for volunteers for anything (not in the bulletin, either). A church never has to whine and plead. The Holy Spirit is committed to giving gifts to His church which will abundantly fill every need.* Relying on His promise, those concerned can pray in private for the right ones to come forward and volunteer. Or they can pray for wisdom to discern gifts in their fellow believers and then ask qualified people. Even the smallest churches can believe God!

Can you put away your squirt gun entirely? Happy fire-tending.

---

* Obviously, if He doesn't supply a particular gift for *your* church, He must not consider this a need.

43

A WORSHIP SERVICE
REALLY CAN BE WORSHIP
That pew
can become holy ground.

"I've never adored the Lord before," said a longtime Christian at a conference recently. There were tears in her eyes. "I've attended worship services all my life, but I never worshiped until today."

Christian, it's up to you, when you come to church, to worship. Nobody can do it for you. All those helps—hymns, prayers, sermons—lead you to the water, but they can't make you drink.

You, personally, must lift your heart to God. *"How can I please You today, Father?"*

Surely by first confessing your sins. You are unworthy to come into His presence! In Acts 3:19 Peter said so earnestly, not to heathen, but to God's people: "Now change your mind and attitude to God and turn to him so he can cleanse away your sins and send you wonderful times of refreshment from the presence of the Lord."

Be specific, *"Father, I'm so sorry that this morning I blew my lid. . . ." "So-and-so was my fault."*

Does this bring to mind an apology you owe somebody? Could you even slip out of your pew and make it right before church begins? Matthew 5:23,24: "If you are standing before the altar in the Temple, offering a sacrifice to God, and suddenly remember that a friend has something against you, leave your sacrifice there beside the altar and go and apologize and be reconciled to him, and then come and offer your sacrifice to God. . . ."

Right on! Leave your offering envelope with an usher just in case the apology takes longer and you don't get back!

And what's worship all about? It's admiring God. Do you do that? Worship is a muscle that is so little used, most of us don't know how. Tell God how wonderful He is by every fresh, innovative way you can.

If perchance you ask a group of Christians in a prayer meeting to offer God worship (as far as I can tell, it doesn't happen very often!), they'll probably turn it into thanksgiving: "Thank You, Lord, for being so kind to me . . ." and they've turned the spotlight onto themselves again.

How about adoration the way Song of Solomon does it? "You are so beautiful. . . . You're a lily among thorns. . . . You're a sachet of myrrh. . . ."

Tell God, "Oh, my Father, you are. . . ." and fill in the blank! Discipline your concentration on who He is and what He does. Not necessarily what He does for *you* (see how God describes Himself in Job 38—41), just what He does, in His matchless wisdom and power.

Think of adjectives that describe Him. Nouns that describe Him. Maybe go through the alphabet, an initial for each.

Concentrate on God—stretch your mind. Adore Him.

Lord, this church service is for You. I'm here to give You pleasure.

44

AN ALTERNATIVE
TO CHURCHGOING
**You don't *have* to sit
through a worship service. . . .**

Instead, select a secluded room where you can take a brother or a sister and go pray through the service. Pray with one eye on the clock:

Pray for the ushers as they're seating the people. . . .

Pray for a great spirit of anticipation over the congregation. . . .

Pray for the organist in his prelude. . . .

Pray for the latecomers.. . . .

For the choir. . . .

The other up-fronters. . . .

The pastoral prayer. . . .

The hymns. . . .

The anthem. . . .

The visitors, the seekers, the troubled. . . .

Pray back and forth in conversational prayer straight through the service, sermon and all.

The word will spread; the group may grow; the service will greatly gain in power—so will the sermon.

They say that when Charles Spurgeon preached, there were 500 in the basement praying for him.

No wonder he was some preacher. . . .

45

THAT EXCITING SCRIPTURE READING
Who knows—
maybe it will punch a hole in the sky.

When our family lived in England a few years ago we often tramped around the wonderful old churches there. I remember particularly one little country church, many centuries old, with its Gothic proportions and its damp, mossy stone . . . , this church had a surprise for us.

Here was the big front door for everyone to go in. Well, no, not everyone. Over to the left was a slot in the outside wall like a letter drop. It was called the "lepers' squint"! Oh, dear God, couldn't all Your children go into church?

No, the ones with leprosy huddled around the slot in the wall and took turns peering through. How precious each turn must have been! One leper might get in on 5 percent of the second hymn, 35 percent of the offering being taken; then it was time to move over.

Let's try it over his left shoulder; maybe I can see a bit more. But that's the end of the slot; let's try the right. Nope, somebody else got there first. What was that last sentence? What did he say? Bless their hearts, what a way to worship God.

You're wondering what this story has to do with Scripture reading in church. Stick with me; it will fit soon.

Think about the whole universe—all of creation—every atom of it jammed, crammed with wisdom, morality, beauty, joy. The morning stars sing together. One moment of time stands shoulder to shoulder with the next moment for a duet. Righteousness, space, truth, and time superimpose, synchronize, flow. How can we figure it? How can our heads get it all together?

God chooses for now to give us just a few brief clues: enough to know we must accept and love and worship Jesus Christ—plus only a few other mouth-watering glimpses into what the whole thing is about.

And all the clues, all the glimpses are in His one Book. His "lepers' squint"!

Now, think about it. All Christ's people gather together on a Sunday morning, and this Book is going to be read from.

(Oh, Minister! Study it in advance. Underline key words for emphasis. Practice it out loud.)

In the special, Holy Spirit atmosphere of Jesus' presence among His gathered people, here comes the high point of the service: we're going to squint through those brief, few words at God's Everything.

People, all of us, listen! *What's He saying? What did He mean by that last sentence? Don't go so fast, Pastor; we're not getting it.*

God!

Vastness is behind Your words! Seas crashing, solar systems roaring,—and the Cross, the Cross!

Read it over, Pastor. What was that again?

46

A SERMON DOESN'T HAVE TO BE
ALL AT ONCE
Teaching situations
need all the ingenuity they can get.

I'd spoken at a Friday-Saturday retreat for the women of Fourth Presbyterian Church in Washington, D.C. On Sunday I slipped into a pew to worship there. (That's a lively, strategic, cleansing place.) In the evening service Pastor Dick Halverson preached half his sermon. Then he sat down, and we stood up and sang a while. Then we sat down, and he stood up and finished his sermon.

Why not? "The mind can absorb only as much as the seat can endure."

———————

Lake Avenue Church recently put together Romans 8 and Bach* for its morning service. After a few preliminaries, our minister of music, whose heart beats as one with Ray's and who works hand-in-glove with him, explained that our worship that morning would be di-

* Selections from his cantata, "Jesu, Priceless Treasure."

vided into three parts—three sections of the eighth chapter of Romans. The sections were printed complete in the Order of Worship.

First Ray preached for about ten minutes on the first section, then the choir sang it. Then Ray preached on the second section, and the choir sang that. Then section three—preached and then sung. Benediction.

Instruction, inspiration, and beauty!

47

PREACHING
It's outside of everybody, even the preacher.

Old Prof Wheeler was the end of an era at Princeton Seminary. He had coached the Barrymores in voice, and when he taught his seminarians to preach, he taught them to *preach*.

After his day, all over the nation the theory came into vogue that preachers were to "share," to get down on the level of their listeners and not come across like some big authority.

Praise the Lord my young husband got in on the end of Prof Wheeler. I can see Ray yet in our little student apartment making his stomach muscles go in and out and practicing bringing his voice up from some unknown depths so he could "project." Did he practice projecting!

First, to people fifteen feet away: "Strike the flagstaff deep, sir knight!"

Then, to people fifty feet away: "Scatter flowers, fair maids!"

Then, to people in the back of some top balcony: "Ho, gunners! Fire a loud salute!"

And then to an imaginary audience across the length of a football field (his shirt really leaving and meeting his belt buckle, and his voice a deep, Shakespearean roar), "Ho, gallants! Draw—your—blades!"

For the first few years Ray preached, every Sunday morning early he was still barking, "Ho! . . . ho!" around the house, as he worked his stomach muscles and thought about where to place his voice so he could project.

The reason? Prof Wheeler's theory was that the preacher *should* come across like a big authority. Why? Not because he is anything in himself, but because his message is the Word of God.

The secret of preaching is for the man to divorce himself from his message. With all the authority of an Old Testament prophet he's to thunder, "Thus saith the Lord!" No "sharing." No apologies.

Then with utter openness and honesty he's to say, "I need this, too. . . . Nobody needs this Word more than I. . . . God had to deal with me this morning before I could preach this to you. . . ."

A man who loses confidence in the Word of God is one who has to "share." His only offering is his own opinion to be considered along with other equally valid opinions. He'd better keep his voice folksy and apologetic—because he may be wrong and he doesn't want to appear perfect, as if he were Mr. Know-It-All.

After all, he doesn't want to *preach at them*. . . .

Have you noticed lately as authority figures have lost stature that the word "preach" has gotten bad connotations? "I don't want to sound preachy, but. . . ."; "Now, I'm not trying to *preach* to you. . . ."

But 1 Corinthians 1 says that to us who are being saved,

preaching is the power of God unto salvation.

"Preach" is a fabulous word. Preaching is full of glory and mystery. Many of the shining moments in Christendom's history have come as the church of Christ sat under the preaching of the Word of God.

Do you disagree that the man must be divorced from his message?

In comic strips a person stands below and his words are printed in a balloon up above.

There you've got it!

The preacher below is, in himself, totally inadequate and totally unworthy. He's got to let the people know he's not the perfect embodiment of the words in that balloon above him. But if that balloon is the preaching of the cross then it's the power of God unto salvation.

In that case, whisper it, shout it, pound it home, take it in, absorb it, treasure it, pass it on, live it out—preacher and people alike.

William Nagenda is a preacher from the heart of Africa. He stood in our pulpit one Sunday morning, tiny and shiny black, and began in his high-pitched voice,

"I said to the Lord, 'O Lord, what shall I tell this people? I feel so dry.' And the Lord said, 'Tell them you are dry.'"

What happened? An electric current of sympathy for William swept through the congregation. (Who hasn't felt dry?) We all began to pray—not for a fabulous African preacher who didn't need any help and who was vulnerable for all judgmental and critical comparisons, but for a small, frail new friend who had to speak when he felt dry. His honesty had disarmed us and won us.

William Nagenda preached long and vigorously, with

such conviction and power that few of us will ever forget it. The frail man below had separated himself from the balloon above. The Word of God was freed to be full of power and authority.

Without that separation a preacher has two choices. He can shout and swagger, hide his personal failures, cultivate admirers and become a fraud. Or he can admit his humanness, try to be just "one of the boys," and share his uncertainty as a blind man leading the blind.

There is another alternative, "I'm not much but, friends, what I have to say is life or death. I need it. You need it. Let's receive it together. 'O earth, earth, earth, hear the Word of the Lord!' "

There's just one requirement: you'd better study the Book all week long. Make sure that in the balloon there's only God's Word, and not yours.

48

**TURNING AWAY
FROM THE MIRROR
Take a look at James 1:22-25
for the picture.**

Somewhere I heard the story of the fellow who overslept and came rushing up the steps of the church just as another fellow was coming out.

"Is the sermon over?" he puffed.

"No, it's just beginning," was the answer. "Now we're going out to do it."

Response is the name of the game. The first ten minutes after a sermon are crucial to whether the seed falls on good ground and takes root and changes lives, or whether birds immediately pick it up and fly off forever.

What are your people going to *do* as a result of what they've *heard*?

This burden is no doubt what gave birth to the "invitation." An invitation gets unbelievably wearisome if it's the only thing a pastor knows to do, Sunday after identical Sunday. It's a great device if used sparingly along with many other techniques.

Once when Ray preached on forgiveness, he asked us to write down on paper our individual "worst sins." He waited in quiet as we thought and wrote. Then he had us write "1 John 1:9" across the face of the whole list, and tear up our papers.

Pastor, perhaps you should ask your flock to write down what they individually resolve to do the coming week, to act on the challenge of God from the sermon.

Perhaps you should ask each one to vow a vow to God to be accomplished by some future date, say three months or six months hence. The church keeps the cards and mails them back on D-date. Each person can check to see if he reached his goal.

Suppose you're exhorting your flock to be encouragers. Then suggest that everyone seek out one person after the service, to whom he'll say, "I love you," "I appreciate you," or "I'm thankful you did so-and-so." Believe me, visitors would stand around thrilled at watching such a display of love. They won't feel left out—just maybe jealous of such a fellowship.

Or instead have them fill out blank cards which have been placed in the pew racks—writing words of love to one brother or sister—which they hand on personally after the service or put in the mail.

Occasionally you might ask them to hold hands and pray for the one on their right and then the one on their left: that God will help them to obey what God suggested to them in the sermon.

Once in a while you might ask them to raise their hands or stand—to receive Christ for the first time or to respond to some Christian challenge.

Once in another while perhaps you'll ask them to step right out of their seats and come forward (no secret hand-raising first lest they feel trapped into some scheme).

Here an altar rail is a wonderful help. Our church has steps across the front which accomplish the same thing. For the physical body to kneel publicly makes a deep impression on one's heart—and a deep impression on others' hearts!

Recently after such an experience a doctor's beautiful wife wrote Ray, "A miracle happened in my life on Sunday, and I want to share it with you. I have been a Christian for a long time, but until Sunday . . . I have never felt cleansed. I needed to physically lay all my sins on the altar and *accept* His forgiveness. . . ."

The Israelite of old personally laid his hand on the head of a sacrificial animal.

Pastor, how long will you keep your people merely listeners, with no choice of action after hearing God's Word but to file out to the tune of a postlude?

49

THE CONCLUSION
OF THE SERVICE
It's time to go.
What a shame.

This is the time to squeeze out the last juices, so that the taste lingers in our mouths.

This is the time to release the perfume that follows us out the door and home.

What's been happening? Continue it.

Did the sermon end full of high victory? Think in terms of a closing hymn and benediction that are short blasts of triumph. Then let the organ sock it to them, fortissimo. Watch people walk out grinning from ear to ear.

Did the sermon end thoughtfully, quietly? There's the cue for minister and organist.

Was the final hymn particularly special? Then why should the choir do their planned choral amen? Instead, the minister of music can point to the final verse of the hymn and they can tenderly repeat it. Then, organist, never mind what the bulletin says your postlude is. Continue that hymn, or play another one on a related subject as the people go.

Sometimes have the choir sing the people out. Sometimes have the people sing themselves out. Keep the theme going somehow right out the door.

Never a dull moment.

Make them sorry it's over—and ready to come back for more.

50

AFTER THE POSTLUDE
Everything depends
on the Monday-to-Saturday span.

The sons of Levi were born into their work. They were enmeshed in worship—as their ancestors had been and as their descendants would be.

We're not like that—but just the same, church up-fronters can't minister heaven to people on Sunday, pick up a paycheck, and live like a child of hell the rest of the week.

To quote the various translations of Romans 6:2, "God forbid." "By no means." "Of course not." "No, no!" "Not at all!" "Never!" "Certainly not!" "What a ghastly thought!"

Consider yourself this way, church musician: you don't "have a church job"; you are a church choir director, organist, or whatever. That's a continuing ministry, for which you need to be a continuing kind of person. (Somehow the pastor's role is more settled; he is the pastor, and that's that. He's *always* the pastor. That's why you can feel free to phone him at two in the morning.)

Friend organist, let's go a step further. Don't be known to the people as just an organist; be known as a godly person. Music isn't where it's at: *God* is where it's at! Music is a great vehicle, but it's only a vehicle, a carrier.

I could improvise on this theme for a long time. No organ number can forgive your sins, graft you into the body of Christ, and promise you an eternal inheritance. There are no fruits of a fugue or a passacaglia, only the fruits of the Spirit. You can be a sour old man or woman behind that instrument.

What am I trying to say?

Well, of course during the week you'll give yourself to hours of hard work in practice; there's no other way. But don't make music your escape. Come out from behind that console, friend, and get where the action is.

Be involved in non-musical activities in the church: get into a small group for Bible study and prayer.

Give yourself away. What can you do to make others happy?

Share your faith with that doubting neighbor. Connect him up with somebody he can sit with in church.

Develop relationships! Love your pastor. Thank God for your choir director. (He's your boss, too, you know.) Be on the team; be loyal. don't even listen to hostile criticism; give your brothers and sisters on the church staff dignity and honor, "for their work's sake."*

Be a Barnabas, an encourager. Instead of expecting people to come to the organ to compliment you, be the aggressor. Thank the soloist; encourage the choir; express

* 1 Thessalonians 5:13.

your appreciation to the choir director, the preacher, and others who serve.

I hate to admit it, but sometimes a minister needs to be faced with this Monday-to-Saturday bit, too. Their profession becomes a game they play, a mask they put on.

How Ray and I shuddered, when early in our ministry a neighboring pastor spent his day off with us and said it sure was fun to get away from his church people for a change so he could relax and cuss and be himself. Poor, poor man.

And I'll never forget the minister's wife whose husband was just about to retire, and she gleefully side-mouthed to me, "I've almost drunk my last damn cup of tea!" Poor, poor woman. What a tragedy. What a waste.

Oh, the exhilaration of being for real! Not of being perfect, but of walking before God! Of ministering before Him, being with others before Him, being alone before Him, working before Him, playing hilariously before Him, eating-sleeping-breathing before Him, with Him, in Him!

Alleluia!

Oh, my Father, what a life!

I stretch out my soul before You and say, "Thanks, thanks, thanks. You're so—SPLENDID!"

51

**SUPPOSE
IT REALLY HAPPENS
After all the blood, sweat and tears,
God comes.**

He descends over all the people like a canopy and together you become aware that you're in a new dimension. You've broken into glory!

I can't describe how it will be for you. It will be different than when He comes to any other group of believers. You will all look like the same old friends to one another, and yet you'll all be different.

There will be a new identification with some of those heavenly scenes in the book of Revelation. Praise will be there, and joy, and new words from familiar lips.

At that moment all the up-fronters need to remember one of Dr. Tozer's stories.

It's the first Palm Sunday, and here comes Jesus riding into Jerusalem on a donkey. The crowds begin to shout "Hosanna! Hosanna!" The old donkey pricks up his ears. Some in the crowd throw their coats in the road; others spread out palm branches.

"Well!" says the donkey, switching a fly off a mange patch. "I had no idea they really appreciated me like this! Listen to those hosannas, would you. I must really be something!"

Friends, if anybody comes around after the service saying, "Wow! That was terrific!"—they're not actually saying hosanna to *you*.

All you did was bring Jesus to them.